Space Vultures!

Karen Ball • Jonatronix

Max's mission log

We are travelling through space on board the micro-ship Excelsa with our new friends, Nok and Seven.

We're on a mission to save Planet Exis (Nok's home planet), which is running out of power. The only way to do this is to collect the fragments that form the Core of Exis – the most powerful energy source in the galaxy.

So far we have collected four fragments, but we need to find a fifth! Only the king and queen of Exis (Nok's parents) know where the final fragment is hidden, so our next task is to find them. It's not easy. A space villain called Badlaw wants the power of the Core for himself.

Fragments collected so far: 4

2

In our last adventure ...

We were on our way to the Planet of Bones, looking for the king and queen, when a strange plant attached itself to the outside of our ship. It was a moon winder.

Ant and Tiger went to investigate but the moon winder trapped Ant! Tiger, Seven and I rescued him, but the moon winder was draining all the Excelsa's power.

We went to Kree-Marr – a planet of plants – and managed to get some help. The Excelsa was free! We are back on course.

Chapter 1 – A hiding place

KAPOW! The Excelsa shuddered, nearly throwing Nok and his friends from their seats.

"We're under attack!" Ant yelled, clutching the side of his control desk.

Max looked out of the viewscreen. A huge energy ball exploded into hundreds of tiny lights in front of them. "It's the Krools!"

Badlaw would stop at nothing to get the final fragment, including sending his robotic army after the micro-friends.

Alarms wailed as Nok pulled on the steering orbs. The Excelsa shot up, just as a second energy ball exploded beneath them.

"There's a meteorite field ahead," Cat said. "Let's hide in there."

"Good idea," said Max. "Take us in, Nok."

Nok steered the ship carefully between the meteorites.

Cat glanced up from her control desk. "My scanners say this is called The Dead Canyon."

"Did you say *The Dead Canyon*?" said Seven, his voice trembling. "Oh, no! That means we've just entered a dead zone."

"What's a dead zone?" asked Ant.

"It is an area where everything gets drained of power," Seven explained.

As he spoke, the friends felt the micro-ship slowing down. The engines spluttered then cut out completely. Everything went quiet as the bridge was bathed in a red glow.

"We're on emergency power," Tiger said.

"Let's hope the Krools have turned back," said Max.

"Never mind about them," Cat said. "How are we going to get out of here?"

"I'm afraid all we can do is wait for a strong space wind to blow us out," answered Seven.

Tiger's watch began flashing a red warning. It meant there was danger close by. "Er, guys ..."

Suddenly a blurred shape shot past the viewscreen.

"There's something out there!" Ant yelled.

Nok jumped out of the pilot's seat and ran to the viewscreen. He stared out at the canyon. Massive flying creatures were swooping towards them. "Space vultures!"

Chapter 2 – Vulture attack

The vultures let out throaty cries as they circled the micro-ship. Suddenly one of them stretched out its long, leathery neck and started pecking the ship.

"We have to stop it!" Max shouted over the knocking noise. "It will break the ship apart!"

The pecking was getting louder and louder, as more and more vultures joined the attack.

Space vultures

Information

Space vultures are aggressive alien birds that nest on meteorites. It is very rare to see a lone space vulture as they always hunt in groups called 'screeches'. They are known as the scavengers of space. If you see a space vulture, get away ... fast.

Diet

Vultures feast on any unlucky spaceships that fly by.

Habitat

Vultures live in colonies in The Dead Canyon and in other meteorite fields.

hooked beak ●●○○○○

bald, purple head ●●○○○○○○○○○○○○○○○○○

bright feathers ●●○○○

strong claws ●●○○○○○

Finding food

Space vultures have very strong beaks. They use them like tin-openers to pierce metal spaceships, as they look inside for tasty morsels. Vultures have strong stomach acid that can dissolve metal.

Chapter 3 – A cunning plan

"The vultures aren't our only problem," said Cat. "The Krools are back again!"

Through the viewscreen the friends could see the Krools' ship looming nearby.

"They *did* follow us into the canyon after all!" yelled Tiger.

"It looks like their ship is losing power, too," said Seven. "They're slowing down."

The loud pecking noise suddenly stopped and the bridge fell silent. The vultures stopped attacking the Excelsa and flew towards the Krools' ship.

"For once the Krools might do us a favour," said Nok. "Their ship is a much bigger target than ours."

"Ha! Serves them right for following us," cried Tiger. "Go feast on that ship, vultures!"

The Krools' ship started to whine and a bright light glowed at the front of it. The vultures backed away.

"What are the Krools doing now?" Max said, looking at the viewscreen.

Seconds later he gasped as a flash appeared from the enemy ship.

WHOOSH! An energy net shot out from the Krools' ship, glowing bright green against the darkness.

The net looped round the legs of one of the fleeing vultures. The creature immediately began to struggle.

"It's trying to get free, the poor thing," said Ant sadly.

The vulture screeched. The more it struggled, the more the net twisted.

"I don't understand," Cat said. "What do the Krools want with a space vulture?"

The vulture flapped its wings, trying to get away. Slowly it began to move forwards, eyes bulging with the effort.

"I get it," Ant said, turning pale. "The Krools are using the space vulture to drag their ship over to ours."

Max saw Ant was right. The Krools' ship was attached to the net with an energy rope. "They're going to attack!" he yelled.

Chapter 4 – To the escape pods!

Tiger ran towards the transit-tube.

"Where are you going?" asked Cat.

"I've had an idea," Tiger replied. "Max, I might need some help."

Max sprinted after Tiger. As the doors on the transit-tube slid shut, Max turned to his friend. "What's your plan?" he asked.

"The escape pods don't need power from the ship. They run on their own power," Tiger explained. "If we fly out and free the vulture, then the Krools won't be able to attack us!"

"How can we do that?" asked Max.

"We can melt the energy net with the pods' thrusters," he answered.

"Well, we've got nothing to lose," said Max.

Max and Tiger each scrambled into an escape pod and sealed themselves inside. Then the escape pods rolled forward. Tiger pressed a button and the ship's exit hatch slid open. He nodded at Max, who gave a thumbs-up signal. Max felt his stomach lurch as his pod dropped into the vast space canyon.

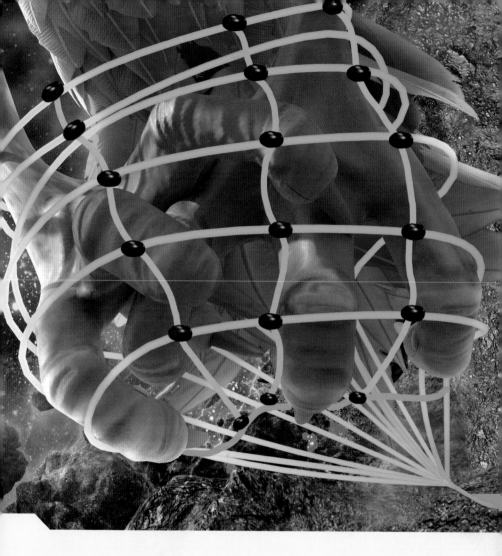

Ahead of them, the energy net glowed brightly in the darkness. The vulture was beating its wings in a desperate attempt to get free. Its loud shrieks echoed round the canyon.

Tiger took the lead and steered towards the frightened bird, dodging the massive boulders in their way.

Chapter 5 – Freedom!

The space vulture gave a loud squawk when it saw the escape pods approaching. It snapped angrily at them.

Max and Tiger both put on a burst of speed to avoid the bird's massive beak. Tiger zoomed off one way and Max the other.

Time was running out. The vulture was dragging the Krools' ship closer and closer to the Excelsa.

Tiger looked at the monitor next to him. "Max!" he said, through the communi-screen. "My power's running low."

Max's voice crackled back through the pod's speaker. "Mine too. We need to act now!"

They sped behind the vulture to the back of the energy net.

Tiger turned his pod around. He reversed until his thrusters were almost touching the sizzling green strands of energy rope. Max quickly copied him.

"Let's blast this net apart!" shouted Tiger.

Both boys revved their engines. A burst of blue energy shot from each of the pods.

The net started to sizzle and hiss. Slowly, it began to fray.

A strong, burning smell filtered into the escape pods.

The vulture tugged forwards and, suddenly, the net snapped. It sounded like a stretched elastic band pinging. The space vulture was free! It beat its powerful wings and soared away to safety.

The plan had worked, but Max and Tiger had no time to celebrate. As they turned towards their ship, Max saw a swirling mass of dust approaching. It looked like a tornado.

"We need to get back to the Excelsa," he said to Tiger. "Now!"

Chapter 6 – Power boost

Max and Tiger swooped up into the Excelsa and the hatch slid shut behind them.

They quickly jumped out of the escape pods.

"We need to get to the bridge and warn the others!" cried Max, already heading to the transit-tube.

"There's a tornado coming!" cried Max, as he ran on to the bridge.

"What!" said Cat. "What are we going to do?"

"There's nothing we *can* do," said Nok, "the power's still out."

"Wait," said Seven, thoughtfully. "The tornado could actually be a good thing. It could carry us out of the canyon."

"Let's hope you're right, Seven," replied Max, taking his seat. "Everyone, brace yourselves."

The noise outside the ship grew as the howling tornado got closer. The ship shook and began to spin as it was caught up in the swirling dust.

"Nok, get ready to power up!" Max called above the noise.

Nok concentrated hard, ready to take control as soon as they were out of the dead zone.

The micro-friends all held their breath. It was their only chance.

The micro-ship tumbled over and over like a pebble caught in a wave. At last it was thrown clear of The Dead Canyon.

The lights flickered back into life and the engines roared. With full power restored, Nok took the ship forward once more towards the Planet of Bones.

Find out what happens next in _The Planet of Bones_.